A BRIEF GUIDE TO
NEWT SCAMANDER
AND THE BEASTS

A Running Press® Miniature Edition™

Printed in China

ISBN 978-0-7624-6072-4

Published by Running Press Book Publishers,
An Imprint of Perseus Books, LLC,
A Subsidiary of Hachette Book Group, Inc.
2300 Chestnut Street
Philadelphia, PA 19103-4371

www.runningpress.com

NEWT SCAMANDER

(EDDIE REDMAYNE)

NIFFLER

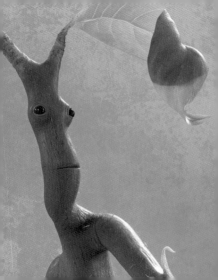

BOWTRUCKLE

THUNDERBIRD

SWOOPING EVIL

ERUMPENT

DEMIGUISE

OCCAMY

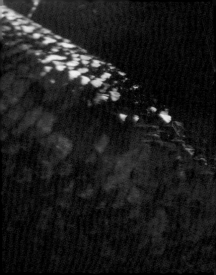

MURTLAP

GRAPHORN

MOONCALF

This book has been bound
using handcraft methods
and Smyth-sewn
to ensure durability.

Designed by
T. L. Bonaddio.

Edited by
Cindy De La Hoz.

The text was set in
Busorama, Fontastic Beast,
and Bodoni Old Style

DO NOT MIX OLD AND NEW BATTERIES.